Ordinary Substance

Ordinary Substance

Zayra Yves

Magdalena & Co.
Santa Clara, CA

Ordinary Substance
Copyright © 2007 by Zayra Yves

All rights reserved. No part of this book may be used or reproduced by any means, graphic, electronic or mechanical, including photocopying, recording, taping or by any information storage retrieval system without the written permission of the publisher except in the case of brief quotations embodied in critical articles and reviews.

Manufactured in the United States of America
Library of Congress Control Number: 2008920738
ISBN: 978-0-6151-8008-3
Third Edition

Publisher: Magdalena & Co. Santa Clara, CA

Back Cover Photo: Zayra Yves by Kurt Loeffler
www.loefflerphoto.com

Front Cover Photo: Sexy Woman © Nikitu
Dreamstime.com

Cover Design: Zayra Yves
Contact the author: www.zayrayves.com

Other Books & Audio Collections by Zayra Yves:

Empty as Nirvana
Crowned Compassion
Sleep in the Sea Tonight with Me

for Natori & Auguste

*may the magic of love illuminate your journey
and your hearts be full of stars*

Acknowledgements:

Of special note, I wish to thank Bill Harris for his amazing support and generous spirit in helping promote my poetic arts, as well as for sharing it generously with others. In addition, I would like to thank Denise Abergel for finding me and sharing my audio poetry collections with Bill at Centerpointe (www.centerpointe.com). I wish to thank Jade Luna for the terrific and intense spiritual support (www.hiddenmoon.com). In addition, I would like to thank Nagi Chami for providing my work schedule with flexibility that only a fellow artist could understand as necessary. It is with love that I am deeply grateful to Eric Galpine and my children for their patience with the long hours that are dedicated to my art. I am also grateful to the rest of family for their faithful commitment to supporting my creative spirit, as well as their continued dedication to living an honest life from the heart. I value their love, patience and loyalty. It is important that I offer thanks also to those who no longer travel with me in body but who remain with me in spirit eternally. I offer gratitude to them for they are powerful teachers, even my most painful foes and my deepest heart breaks have thus shed light on the core of Being and timeless love, so without them this book could not exist. Last but not least, I wish to thank you for purchasing this book and supporting the arts. I hope it will touch you, move your spirit and inspire you to reach for the heavens within your soul.

Before you awaken to what you are,
ten thousand words
and a myriad of spiritual experiences
will not be enough.

After you awaken,
just one is too much.

Adyashani

Contents:

Forward by Bill Harris

I. open the hand of silence

Into the River	18
Dreaming of Water	
The Day My Body Left Me	20
Cult of Contemporary	
Becoming Abstract	22
Not Waiting	
Broken Pieces of Light Still Shine	24
The Seeker Has Stopped Seeking	26
Bodies of Angels	28
Karma	30
Cotton Mouth	
Elephant Song	32
Lions Rattle the Night	
A state beyond sorrow…	34
The Dream that Love Sent	36
Snapped Loose	

II. not contained by anything

Zodiac in a Jar	40
In the Cave	
Rummage	42
Closed Circle	
At 2:30 in the morning…	44
Attachments	
Immaculate Deception	46
Dead Right	
Guarded Affection	48
Fugitive Desire	
Some Kind of Sabotage	50
Shake the Spiritual Tree	
Abandoned	52
On the Subway with an Outcast	
Un-tame	54
Meeting Samsara	
Orphaned	56
New Age Laundry	
This is How God Smokes You	58
Inversion	

Enlightenment in the Time of Clichés   60
Awareness Doesn't Need Permission   62
Innocence

III. more than one way to carry water

Time   66
Night
Memento   68
The Opium of You
Insecurity   70
Houdini's Handcuffs
Narcissus   72
Punch Line
Smallest Particle of Matter   74
Possession
They Owe Nothing   76
Fallen Stars
What Cannot Rest in Peace   78
Letter to Ramses
What I was not counting on…   80
Little Nun Finch   82
Thrust of Sky
The Poem Your Mother Warned You About   84
When No One is Watching
Sheba's Song   86
Your Name
Captive   88
Reclaiming the Body
O Yes to the Wild   90
Discovering Agamemnon   92
Temple Dancing
In Your Tavern Eyes   94
Hymn to Osiris
To Wake Before Extinction   96
Horseshoe Grace
Musician   98
Eros in Waiting
Epitaph   100
Changing Positions of Light
Clay Twist of Face   102
Fragrance
Twilight   104
Bittersweet

VI. flowers plucked from the road

From the Center	108
Sudden	
Supple as the Wind	110
Wishing Tree in Delhi	
Here	112
No Pity in This Poem	
Panoramic	114
Courage	
Damaged Poetry	116
Impressionism	118
Still Life: Oil on Linen	
Autumn	120
Island Goddess	
Following the Stars Home	122
For the living:	
Soft Cusp	124
Overture	
Pilgrim Hitchhiking on the Road of Life	126
When I Die	128
A Blind Path	
At Ugly's Saloon	130
Healing Hands	
Ban-cha (toasted green tea)	132
Situational Perspective	
Speed of Love	134
The Great Wall of China	
Street Monk	136
Just This, Only This	
Dissolving	138
Translucent	
Pinholes	140
The Heart Moves into the Body	
Journey of the Magi	142
And, it was going to rain…	144
Village Stories	
After Midnight	146
Sanctuary	
The Perfect Poem	148

❧ Forward by Bill Harris ❧

Poets and mystics have much in common. They deal with the ineffable, the mystery, which cannot be expressed. The 5th Century Chinese sage, Lao Tzu, begins his famous spiritual classic, the *Tao te Ching*, by describing the ineffability of reality:

*The tao that can be told
is not the eternal Tao
The name that can be named
is not the eternal Name.*

Later, he says:

*Look, and it can't be seen.
Listen, and it can't be heard.
Reach, and it can't be grasped.*

Nonetheless, Lao Tzu wrote 81 verses describing what cannot be described, ending with the words:

*True words aren't eloquent;
eloquent words aren't true.
Wise men don't need to prove their point;
men who need to prove their point aren't wise.*

What then qualifies as "ineffable?" And if something truly is ineffable, why do human beings keep trying to express it? This urge must have something to do with the fact that humans are social beings—and natural chatterboxes. We feel compelled at least to try to tell others what we feel and experience.

The fact is if we didn't try to express that which cannot be expressed, we'd have to be silent. When you get right down to it, *every* experience, *every* feeling, is ineffable—nothing that happens can ever really be explained. Attempts to describe even the briefest moment of existence miss the mark.

Why? Because life is an infinite, multi-dimensional flow; everything happens all at once with each interconnected bit affecting everything else, always changing, always dancing, never sitting still—a giant hall of mirrors where everything reflects everything reflecting everything.

For that reason, any description is but a skeleton of the real thing. Thousands of words cannot adequately describe even the briefest—and most mundane—of experiences.

Yet we try.

Buddhists say that attempts to describe reality are but "a finger pointing at the moon." It's the moon that's important, not the finger. A true poet then is one who points at the moon in such a skillful manner that even that which cannot be described—even the infinite multidimensional nature of reality, the ungraspable mystery of existence—is somehow recognized and experienced.

The truly talented poet somehow triggers a part of you that already knows the moon. It sees the finger, feels the moon, and says, "Yes."

Zayra Yves is such a poet—a poet with the most unimaginably skillful pointing finger. Whether you experience her on the printed page as in this magical little book or from her own lips as with one of her enchanting CDs or in one of her public performances, her words evoke something in you that cannot be expressed or described. She may speak to something with which you are well acquainted or introduce you to parts that were hidden until she invited them into your awareness.

Either way, the energies of Life will be stimulated, and you will be better for the experience.

Whether she speaks of love and passion, or pain and the mystery behind all human experience (for Zayra is a mystic in the truest sense of the word), her words will speak to a place deep inside of you that once called, awakens—and once awakened, changes you forever.

I once told my students that Zayra's poetry would make their toes curl. I should have said that it would make their souls curl.

So, turn the page and let Zayra Yves guide you to the mystery that is you, the mystery that cannot be described but which with the proper guidance can be known.

The Tao is like a well:
used but never used up.
It is like the eternal void:
filled with infinite possibilities.

Bill Harris
November 23, 2007
www.centerpointe.com

open the hand of silence

There should not be any particular teaching.
Teaching is in each moment...
                    Suzuki Roshi

Into the River

I do not deny
there is an old face
within me
willing to be erased

I fall as a stone
into rebirth

Dreaming of Water

In the land of bones
without rain…

I do not mourn what is lost
or seek answers to abate loneliness.

My skin sheds as the faces
of wood rot and change
charred from suffering
decomposed and mute.

The sky is blank
and the winds offer nothing
to translate

as layers of myself
scarred and unblinking
fall into epiphanies,
spend the night in footprints
and dream of water…

*it   must   be   here
under   the   surface   somewhere.*

The Day My Body Left Me

she packed everything
and was gone without a note

I already knew she was going
and I had it coming

she was tired
of the segregation

it was no secret
she was fed up with the abstract
nonsense of trying to relate
to concepts of divinity
and borrowed forms of God

all she wanted was
a real experience

burning in the bones
of a truth that is on fire with life

Cult of Contemporary

Inside a seeker is the hunt
to find the bitter, the nimrod
and the red wheelbarrow
with a creative mannequin
who points a bald finger
toward some drunk moment
where uncertainty invades
the mind dressed as a trendy doll
stained and torn in the corner
like a self help book
marked and folded too many times
by a misguided miracle
that got lost on page eleven
between the earnest and a mudfish
chapter of twenty ways to lose
between the black and white
that spread gray all over
the world to march a fine line
of separation and awakening.

But never mind all that
because being dead has never been
more in style.

Becoming Abstract

It is a trend. A movement.

Before you think too much about it
an accent lands where it does not belong
like more of a bee sting
or a train at 1 AM
and not at all what you planned.

Suddenly it is an indistinct color
or some loose phrase about Van Gogh
lost in what tried to be lucid -
that weak attempt to lure the awkward.

Or your mind stops motionless
which seems terribly odd considering
how absurdly obsessed it is with itself
full of spray paint, dope
and burning flowers.

Then the body is smashed to the floor
in the desire for perfect skin
that feels smooth as madness
where the delicate don't actually break
and hope wanders around
not fully known.

Now in light of all that
(and generally speaking)

*I prefer to be touched
more often...*

        don't you?

Not Waiting

I am not waiting for the world to love me back.

Yeah, I know I have heard about that idiot compassion
and how not to love too much or be a burning saint.

It is true that skulls hang from roofs, bones dance
in the streets; people shoplift, beg and grow moss.

The news is crazy with itself. It foams at the mouth
wears the best clothes; is unrepentant for all the darkness.

It is rumored that the succulent and juicy are for sale
sort of like a fruit no one seems to get enough of.

And, even though everyone keeps saying this is IT,
the end of everything, the end of the world;

that we should scrape, bite and chain smoke…
somehow I believe that even a star killed by clichés

recovers its light in the blank void of somewhere.
It sort of reminds me of where I am going

even though I only vaguely remember that place,
sort of sovereign but unsolved and unnamed

like lips pressed to lips when we turn silent
to be near the scent of loving one another.

Maybe sometimes we just don't know how to love
in the absence, in the moment, in return…

Broken Pieces of Light Still Shine

The trouble is it goes on and on
like this:

    the birth and death of "almost"
    minus the particulars and never as careful.

In the time since we have parted:

    they have dethroned a planet,
    forced a dark god into a fragmented myth
    and assigned Hell another hole
    on the third quadrant of the moon.

After the zero eclipse of celebrated silence:

    I consider the language of fireflies,
    jeweled squid and lantern fish
    a sign that it is possible to use light
    to communicate and expose indifference.

Another day without apologies:

    in the shadows of reptiles and bats
    cruel thoughts gnaw and bite
    but the red eared turtles lavishly court each other
    and the pandas are faithful;
    so, I am letting go of everything
    that has hurt

            { all of the ruin }

for what remains lunar
undiscovered
and fertile in possibility...

to become the Universe of one.

The Seeker Has Stopped Seeking

I am not fascinated by the latest fashion
or the best mustard.

I don't really want to know
if you travel alone
or parade through hundreds
to purchase peace
or buy potions of erotic juices
from a holy caravan.

Life doesn't have to entertain me.

My journey begins in a drum beat,
right up inside the leg
where the vein is rhythmic

into the chambers of my hips,
torso, ribs, sternum, neck, lips
and round again.

It is the tiger in my bones
stealth as it arrives…

like the moment you
look into my eyes and
stop questioning it.

Unguarded I sway
in the fine sand of faces -
no longer waiting
for the wind to call or translate.

This afternoon is full of shapes
that have meaning…
my body has gone soft in the chest

everything changes the minute
love shows up.

Bodies of Angels

fall from heaven deep into the sub lunar sea
unknown are their crimes, names or choices to leave

they wash ashore alabaster, agate, free
without feathers, without testimony

all that remains is the shape off their flight,
an archway of dreams upside down in double V's

an outline of wings from the center of their backs
wrinkled skin in translation between water and air

between transparent of nothing yet solid as light
who lands as jelly fish, slime opalescent and beached

these fallen angels who ride on thunder clouds
by chariots of rain, of storm, of lore

and wait for their voices of transmutation while ancestors
shake the rattles, cast healing bones in a circle

of stones guided by magicians, holy men and ghosts who
emerge from the caves, cliffs, from land, from Morro Rock

we wait for our names to be blessed, then spoken in the native
tongues of whales, dolphins and starfish who gather as

a wave breaks illumination onto the shore, as it breaks we
open our bloodless hearts and light shines into our eyes

we remember being born, dying, falling…remember
rising again on this same shore, a beach of bodies

our salty hearts are torn from shells, first with a push
a howl, then by pause, by a hush as life arrives pink

through the nose then spreads to the chest in a moan
as the newly born lose their wings, open their eyes

raise their heads in this world of strange beauty
as our voices emerge from song of hope and the brave

Karma

I am listening to you after the laughter
as one listens to sleep

I hear you after the storm
as one hears tiny feet on the floor

I am listening to you after the passion
as one listens to the silence of a cut tree

I hear you after the glass breaks
as one hears an embrace

I am listening to you after death
as one listens to the sea

Cotton Mouth

The teacher pulled the petal
from the blossom
with a pinch
so quick that no one noticed
how easy it was
to break the vine of light
from the limb
until they were parched
and choked on his reasons
for enlightenment.

Elephant Song

keeper of tears
between earth and sky
from the desert to the sea
right in the curve of an hour
full of gray, yet calm
           she journeys the length
           of your heart
without a compass
or the luxury of faith
at the crossroads
she reminds you
under the shade of a tree
to remember in silence

           the bones of value
           the soul of feeling

   all that is worthy

Lions that Rattle the Night

The mind is fire
released from the skull
by the sound of lions
that roar into the darkness
as if they do not weigh
the heart for virtue
or gather the knowledge
of holy things
they walk among the stars
with their feet on the ground
and every living thing stops
what they are doing,
even those in the middle
of raw love
to listen to their truth.

A state beyond sorrow…

is in the land of Bodhisattva
without fences of criticism
or houses of attainment.

It is prime real estate
that does not provide churches
graveyards or grocery stores

no airports, trains or
fancy clothes.

Simply enter the water
naked as a vessel of wisdom.

The Dream That Love Sent

He came to me from the mysteries...

first in a dream from a far off land
where the dead are wrapped in linen
and prepared during life to live again.

He came from the waters of ancestors
ancient wonder, dust and isolation.

At noon as a message on a desk, he came
inside a world of rules and paper clips.

*Pale skin with his eyes full of light
and clear as the desert sky on Sunday...*

he came half dressed in socks
to find me in a box, half open, in a glimpse
he called me from the winding halls
lured me from sleep.

*Open hearted without tears
like a soul shaped in a Mandala
that circle of fire burning from within...*

He arrived naked and naked we kissed
for the first time to let the silence rest
let the unexplained fall away
and the living full live.

Naked we dove into the waves of a song
to swim hand in hand to the land of our birth;
we followed the sound of a distant prayer
in silken cord, jelly fish and sand dollar.

He came to me like that: fragrant, pure,
full as gardenias, peaceful in love again.

We became light swimming toward more light…

Snapped Loose

Being safe was so safe
that I did not want to part with it
even if it was colder than hell

or take the risk
to get lost in a new language
that could resurrect the heart
from its asylum
and give me a second chance.

But here I am
rising out of my personal inferno
stripped of all belief
with a core that is empty of omens
and a prison door wide open

to witness all the moons
I held hostage
snap loose like total lunatics
(those wild lovers
 of the mystical Divine).

I wish I would have surrendered
and forgiven
a whole lot sooner.

not contained by anything

*Barefoot and naked of breast, I mingle
with the people of the world.*
Ch'an

Zodiac in a Jar

You tease and mock
my fascination with the heavens
and the stories that fall
from the sky.

Listen, this is how it is:

I collect stars in a jar
to remind me that we exist
auspiciously in all things
from lip to celestial.

The broken sun:
a 1,000 jagged pieces and shards
spread across the universe
to be born again.

Anyway, I have seen you
sleeping like a village poem
wrapped in colors of innocence
or sometimes posing as Apollo.

So, you won't
talk me out of gathering
the remains of a splintered sky.

I will even save room
on the bottom
for the fractured glory
of your styled cynicism.

In the Cave

They saw visions
heard voices, opened portals
danced in circles, called upon symbols…
desperate, foolish and greedy.

I envied them.

For I saw nothing, heard nothing
no matter how deep my breath
or how sweet the mantra;
no matter what thoughts broke
from the shores of my mind…

I was nothing inside something
that did not have a name

it was not empty
it was not full

neither broken or whole
the same as a stone that falls
from inside a cave wall
to land on its knees.

Rummage

In the junk drawer
I cannot find what I want.

The tender angels
have disappeared.

What is left?

Tacks, leaking ball points
and strands of hair
mixed with the dust
of old receipts
and no one to translate.

Closed Circle

It has no need for love,
for there is nothing outside of itself
to love. It is a closed circle
of self-prorogation.

In the absence of suffering
it has no waste,
no absolute cycle of being born
or dying or living off
its own excretion.

No air to breathe.
Nothing goes out or comes in.
No sway of the womb.
No shock of the penis.

Of its own design it is made
self-sufficient, fertilizing itself
with the primitive maw
that spins on a wheel of ambivalence.

It has no desire for you
for you cannot complete
what is whole unto itself
a symbol unconscious.

At 2:30 in the morning....

unhappiness argues with itself
and sends a cool visitor in darkness
that paces back and forth
in a still room

to gnaw at the mindless chatter
as it moves inside the skin
like ants into the bones with threats
of a starless night

Attachments

In the background static
marginal, peripheral and on the edge
of my limits.

You hide behind the lenses
of permanent nouns that subsist
on counterfeit visions
in the tick of Self-impish
while I aim to throw myself madly
in all directions
and escape the sinkhole
of average.

Immaculate Deception

Do not emphasize any point in particular
just be sure to punctuate
the missing emotions dumped
in a back alley
as the murdered body
of yourself -
the one you killed
but blamed on someone else.

Come on
be rude and throw all your dishes
against the wall -
break the windows
destroy the mirrors.

Welcome the shattering
of your holy unholy face.

It is time to confess,
to get real…
no one was there
except you.

Dead Right

We cut out what was faithful
and used the blunt edge of opinions
to remove consciousness
from the bone.

But first we stalked truth
took it hostage
and slashed it to ribbons
with questions.

Nothing was left
except a ravaged corpse
bleeding in the light.

Guarded Affection

another cold word
   is detached

    smoothly

        it
           falls

graceful as an autumn leaf
    in love with gravity

out of your mouth
into my ear

      a

    petite

       death

and my captive truth
that last testament of blossom

   dangles

     from

        a withering stem

as lips are erased
   by an unmerciful

        wind

Fugitive Desire

And, suddenly
without a flash of light

supernova
or anything that smells good

I understand
we are beyond death -

that we didn't mean to kill
love with ignorance.

It is just that we cannot find
what or who we seek…

everything we give
and take is conditional.

Some Kind of Sabotage

Reality is poised
in the air
with blue magnolias
waiting to drop
into the murmur of night
like a bandit
that shoots holes
into the heart
year after year
to get even
for mindless words
and spilled light.

Shake the Spiritual Tree

till the fruit of truth falls at your feet
and you cannot speak
because suddenly you realize
the other truth
is a seed of awareness
still clinging to the branch

Abandoned

I am famished and clawing my way
out of your psyche

just so you can slap me
and show me how to survive
in a world that will stain me
with abuse.

I walk with the same hips
and limbs that you gave me.

Then you tell me:

no one cares if you here,
so don't confuse yourself
with miracles.

On the Subway with an Outcast

He is big.
His weight could crush me.

Everyone watches him
from the sides of their eyes
and pretends not to.

The tattoos on his knuckles
spell out a name I cannot read.

Our eyes meet for a moment.

If he were my son
I would name him for a warrior;
for a mountain with strength
like *Modimule (mo-de-mu-lay)*
meaning: *God is Here.*

Un-tame

If you have wished for
my longing…

I cannot give it to you
for I am empty as a dark star
lost in the void.

Meeting Samsara

At the lamp and street sign
of what could have been

I hold my breath
for your narcotic kiss.

I am riveted
in the shapeless dark
less than secrets
and crushed by the poppies
of small gods.

Orphaned

If I could give a name to this feeling
the way I might name a child
maybe it would settle down

stop crying all through the night
and let me hold it
until it fell quiet in my arms.

Somehow it might start to trust
life and smile.

New Age Laundry

all day you wore
the fragrance of awareness
as a second skin

but soon desired
to be free of responsibility
and left it in the sun

an old cotton shirt
on the dirty line
of citrus clean

as if no one knew
you would fold it
behind closed doors

leave it on a shelf
with the threads of ignorance
in a dank closet

This is How God Smokes You

first, he pulls the buds right off the plant
breaks the tiny beads
between his fingers
until they crumble in fine piles
of scattered ovals

with the flat side of his palm
he crushes you along the edge
into a straight line of command
that folds without a sound

your remains
fall into a clean white roll
licked tight

he strikes the fire
and slow burns you
dry to the end

Inversion

peel the lie from this quarrel
and strip your absence from the page
since the beginning
starts in a sprout of words
not more
than the dust of a myth
where forever is the epitaph
that cannot sleep
but turns over in the soil
of what could be

Enlightenment in the Time of Clichés

is a book I carry around
but never manage to read past chapter four.
I try to convince myself
of a new shoreline
or the center of something important –
that there is nothing to fear.

I question Angels
search for gateways into super consciousness
and dig around
in the dusty pits of old stories
and discover wormholes of unknowns
steeped in tea leaves.

Of course, I feel guilty.
What if I have missed the worn skin
of someone dear
or skipped the pages where we fell in love
then drifted into separate villages
torn apart by rage and whiskey?

And, what remains after
I put the book you have become
on the shelf?

I discover the truth is
I am afraid to know who you really are -
who is in the delicate presence
or the art of this moment?

Who is inside their dharma
or lost in the art of flirting with death
and sporting holy tattoos?

Maybe you have already become a bodhi tree
that I mistakenly cut down.

So, I would rather leave enlightenment
between the salted pages
unmapped and stained beyond recollection
eloquently unattainable
than find we are nothing more than
a cliché from pages 27 to 104.

Awareness Doesn't Need Permission

Tonight the room is empty of angels
except those with dirty fingernails
and lopsided coats
in this broken old building
walls are streaked in black tears
stale, full of regret
and brittle
like the women
who sit in termite infested chairs
smell of spearmint gum and cigarettes.

In this orgy of the crude
I remember a sentence I read somewhere
about awareness being present
even when people are not –
it moves through people without their consent
and doesn't need permission…

so, just because they appear to be comatose
catalogued as lunatics
sickened by the aggressive horrors
of some-ism
doesn't mean they are.

After all they are comfortable
at the foot of the hill
living on the hinges of graveyards…

where death is the intimate
companion of wisdom and truth.

Innocence

I lost you
among the jawbones, skulls and tibiae
somewhere in the middle
of a room set aside for mummies
pale ghosts emptied of will
and sarcophagi.

more than one way to carry water

*At our last parting
bending between boat and shore…
that weeping willow.
Shiki*

Time

falls from the tree
and I remember how easy it is
to bruise the promise
of what we are
with what we think
we should be

Night

In a dark hat he wanders
through memory
leaves a glass of water on the stand
wears your chap stick
and smells like a clean shirt.

It is not only that he shares your habits
but that his hands are slender
and manicured to detail
so I begin to imagine you there
palpable and cool.

I start to think that when I roll over
I will look into your eyes
to see how your heart aches
for what matters.

But it is only Night
gone blue with complaints
about the Sun –
that hot fuse with too much passion
burning the edge of reason.

I squint my eyes in the dark
and try to see in that pin prick view
everything I love
except I am deceived again
in the void of you.

Memento

I keep trying to write this poem
where I tell you something important
remind you of places in Africa
and recall the possibility of friendship
like the days when we all took that for grant it
those easy transformations and miracles.

Instead what comes to mind is red
in the scratch of recusant expectations
before it washes away in the river
to swim with conspicuous sun fish.

I watch the clouds shift
and remind myself that nothing returns home
until someone has let it go.

The Opium of You

The opium of you has found me
in the smoke of yesterday
and I can't help but think
now that you have killed off the tomorrows
I might have loved
at least give me the dance of gypsies
and a flower that spreads light.

Insecurity

I have been wearing the image of you
for so long now that I have forgotten myself
thread bare with lost buttons.

I wonder why I accepted second hand attention.
I wish I could remember why I listened
or wanted to dress like you.

It must have been the edge you had -
how I wasn't good enough
or I should have been better

(*if I were just different
  if I were more like you*).

Today I gave up
that false image I too eagerly put on.

Suddenly, I prefer my own skin.

I dress in my own ideas
and I keep my head up as I willow
through the streets without you.

Houdini's Handcuffs

I slip through key holes
unlock secrets while you kneel
for my proclivities.

I have suits, picks and whips
for every dangerous thought
every curious myth.

It makes no difference if it is elusive
I can turn a minute into a slave
name moods like gods.

I navigate the maze of uncertainty.
I am an expert at escape.

So, it was accidental how you
become a cure
for trickery and hoax.

I never expected you
to call me by my true name
trespass every taboo
slip the knot from truth.

I never imagined
I could be unfastened
from the inside out.

Narcissus

Maybe the homeless woman
went to those same clubs in Paris and Prague
smoked that same dope
and tilted her head to the side.

Perhaps she kissed dates like you
lit up on a new wave of intellectualism
like the know-it-alls of Rimbaud and Akhmatova
big with art (all that neon vernacular of passion)
but short on feeling, absent of being.

Probably she danced for awhile in that haze
knew a real bum like you by heart
before she decided to be a voice lost among stars
like the romantic notion of peace.

Punch Line

After we meet, you will want a story.

And, I will try to create one
that doesn't speak of violets
or past loves or how I peaked
in the balance of promised seasons
full of myth against the pillows
like some sort of Eve
on the stone steps of night's door
with the loan of my body
pressed into unanswered questions
heart to heart.

I will skip the tiger swallowtail,
the indigo details of how dreams curve
through translation and just get to
the punch line

where it all falls apart
over scattered bones and prophecies
in that finite second between
dark and light.

Smallest Particle of Matter

In wet darkness
he wants to know how
she could give up
on love?

Not the sort of love
that marries and owns
but the kind
that raises the vibration
and knows
the pulse of the world
as it moves
through the heart.

She feels the taste
of salt rising
but she cannot find
her voice,
so she remains silent
in that vast stillness –

    infinitesimal.

Possession

He travels her body
and ages like any other man.

In the cracks of her skin
he imagines every sort of journey
to an endless line
of gold –
somewhere for a flag pole.

He misplaces parts of himself
inside of her
while he looks for the secret
that is written
just for him.

But she offers him no mystery.

She is greedy and obsessive.
She never returns the man to the man.

And, he does not die
rather he admits simply to himself
that she was nothing more
than a beautiful mirage
in his memory.

They Owe Nothing

far deeper than the glitter in her eyes
or the imagined suffering of
a thousand sleepless nights
she could see that he
like a battered landscape
had doomed himself a prisoner
his empty glass knocked over
to spill bitterness on her dress -
he captures the moment in his own way
swallows the olive, licks the salt
left over from his hotel fantasy
alone with a box of fables
he drifts into the night
searches her face for the keys
to a house he invented
but one she never lived in

Fallen Stars

We were drunk on the cliché
so did not notice

dust on the halo
or the warning in a dream
until the sun crashed
in our window
shattered the bed
with the sound of a train.

After: there was nothing

except a slight blush of purple
in the morning sky -

no one to claim
our bodies of love.

What Cannot Rest in Peace

Nothing is sadder than being buried
in what you used to love
but don't really know enough of
to love anymore.

In that graveyard
is the one relationship that lost its way
followed the wrong idea home
to die
in a pile of confusion
betrayed by circumstances
of its own creation.

The end is a deluge
as silence is pawned
between torn pages
for a half truth, some measure
of worth in stone words
like a battered inscription on a tomb.

Letter to Ramses

For too long the stone of you
has been heavy inside of me.

Of course, I wish death did not require
this much language
or that tangibles didn't escape me.

And, after so much time
I have nothing to go on
except ruins (forgive me)…

I cannot remember dates
or how it is that obscurity
becomes light
only that somehow it is supposed to
parallel beauty.

You have no choice except to be
where history has placed you
and since stones do not give love

I suppose it is time
to pry you loose from my insides.

What I was not counting on…

[*"The voices are lost
         only after their meanings are lost."*]

It is a good thing I did not look for you
to cast your shadow
outside the walls
or leave a map
like a rose on my night table
so, I might follow you…

as a celestial craving
one licks and licks
like sugared martinis
off the lips.

I remember
the first time…
you were extremely hard
to find

as words on a clean white page.

I could not help myself
I wandered
through the names withheld…

understanding of course
that stones do not move stones

or how private truths
can remain etched
in the most unholy place

questions curve
to exhale in a last breath
as if the face speaks
without words...

in circles of smoke
those silent impressions
played in roulette

where the highest risk
is the heart.

I remember your eyes
illuminated with a love
I will never forget

so it is a good thing
I closed mine
just before you left.

[*quote from artist Vincenzo Agnetti*]

Little Nun Finch

Tiny light
of prayer to transfigure
our desolate fears
into faith…

   *please rise
       and sing.*

Thrust of Sky

I demand to know more
because he taught me the substance
of nude stilt.

His fingers from the sea
with rivulets of touch and stingray
swim into my torso.

I have waited for nights like this
with rain on my skin
and he has me

open for the twilight estuary
of sex on our lips that drink
swallow and juice
licking neck and helio
on fire with flavor.

I give myself
in moans of light and arch

for the man who would have me
cry out his name in honor of the sky
he thrusts into me.

The Poem Your Mother Warned You About

Here I am empty handed
with a few ghosts
to embrace the philosophical pillars
of Socrates and Buddha
plus a little of Plath's moodiness
and a shot of Sexton's poison.

It is true I confess
I am a sucker for the wrong poems
drunk on emotion
full of passion and burnt raw to the core.

If it has a hangover, dances for love
with eyes lined in khol
if it was lost in the back alley
abandoned with anonymous diaries

I will fall for it.
I will ask for an autograph.

If it spreads itself too thin
too open
walks through the streets
for that last cigarette
smoked in sin for the untidy joy
and sideways sorrow
rouge of mistakes
dressed in a strange elegance
no one can articulate…

I will probably take it home.

When No One is Watching

All I can offer you is this poem
that would buy you a drink for who you really are
and give you a full body of warmth
that when touched opens
with the perks of small tits.

Sheba's Song

My heart is a vineyard of grapes
ripe and full
waiting patiently in the rain
for the one who will come early
pull tenderly
from the branches
crimson, pomegranate
swollen with purple
intoxicated with the fever
on the juice of new love pulsing
in my breast.

Your Name

is a plume of fire under my skin
by candle light:

San Miguel, Eden, Guadalupe, Mary, Paul

as it falls through the constellations
of violin, piano, flute
in a moment, a turn, a glance…
a touch of hand or an echo outside a window
hidden in darkness like a spy
as an incantation, a moan
that changes direction in the wind
with the tumbleweed song

and travels in the night to find me
as I wait for you
in an exile that is pregnant with potential
and a heart full of forgiveness
like a work of art
in devotional promise

where I wait
for you to emerge
weightless, ethereal, eternal
and unspoiled by this world of form

Captive

My bones are fixed
inside the cage of this body
where the Beloved is perched
in my breast
as the heart tears on love's
promise and falls
on the floor of hope.

Reclaiming the Body

I float like pollen
comfortable with absence
never worrying
where I will land
until
I meet you –

Suddenly
the fragrance of love
rises up to embrace me
and the flowering
beauty of being ordinary
is a star kiss
on the path to Being.

O Yes to the Wild

a starless night
alive with the roar of lions

in a swift movement
of darkness that is not sad
or full of sorrow

bodies curve in tune
to the sounds of dreams

their naked insecurity
is an orchestra of loose notes
that reveal love

emptied of moonlight
verse by verse

Discovering Agamemnon

You arch sideways to defy an ill sun

>bleaching our sight, our hats
>stretched canvas tight, reptilian white.

Here you find the mask you wear:

>a god or a hero;
>a new name for your article
>melting moist on my inner thigh.

Forgetting to take notes

>I prefer the curve of your ear,
>as we drop the bones,
>the tools, and forsake the urn.

Discovering the treasure of a face

>we close the lion's gate
>brush history off these mirror lips
>intoxicated you sing an aria:
>
>>*"this too will turn to dust one day
>>kiss me now, before it is too late."*

Unencumbered is my impulse

>to unbutton the modern circles
>we are in, shed the burdens.

You slip from the line of day

>as insular threads of color
>fall to the floor

    we meet naked in plum nipples.

This mystery we earned.
   I wish to borrow you,

     thieve ancient materials,
     fashion an

        affaire d' amour

              out of body.

Fragrant of rose and sandalwood
   is my slender alabaster figure
   pressing into yours
   flat, then oval.

As if by osmosis the meridian I am
   uncoils into the olive length
   you call:
         "myself"

               buried underground

Temple Dancing

sultry as my hips begin
deliberate in an adagio

this dance I dance for you
bare feet on mosaic tiles
to the rhythm of distant drum
leopard pipe and flute

my body uncoils, unveils
coral hues, sapphire blue

nude you swim in the sutra
lavender skin resplendent
folding itself in pose
and gesture

this bending of light
from one celestial body
by the crystal magnetism
          of another

In Your Tavern Eyes

brewing yeast and seed swirl amber
spilling a circle stain on denim deeds

at full tilt your smile cues the stick
spin the eight ball to the right pocket

hot we electrify thigh to thigh
guess who will be under who

red hand pressed to belly hoop
rocking bluegrass guitar curves

hips a universe of chrome pink
as fingers slide under hook and lace

Hymn to Osiris

Where are you my sweet, my bitter one?

Come to me from the shadows unfold your secrets
your shame, your triumphs, give over your woes.

Make yourself known as a diamond
brilliant in my crown, ruby red in my heart

that I may know you
belt unclasped, armor undone

that I may lay with you
unharmed, unadorned.

Come to me anointed in holy oil
bathed in mercy, of noble flesh…

I will arch my clover wings
spread myself over your body

and fly as a God is resurrected inside.

To Wake Before Extinction

If passion were airborne, waterborne
and contagious as a cold
would you rush into me? Spread
like wildfire, fever…and kiss me?

If hate could be nothing more than a thin
fragile layer
and we didn't have to worry about
Red Tides, Global Warming
or the Ice Age, would you let me
touch you?

Suppose love could restore the dying
Atlantic, the Mediterranean?

Suppose it could restore the song
a dolphin sings?

Maybe a hug is equivalent to a prayer
and gives sight to the blind.

So, why not feel this love I offer you
as a call to return to the forgotten city
across the waves of dreams
as our hearts race to feel each other?

If my love arrives on the sands of your life
I dare you to embrace me...
before I slip back into the sea
cyan as mystery.

Horseshoe Grace

Without a face I am upright, a stump
a marriage of necessity

forgotten in rust, weathered
unintentional
I was created without limbs.

I am plain, easily mistaken
as I stand totem
for those who cannot, who do not
possess the glitter of worldly charm.

On the sidelines
I am the ordinary thing,
the lock one must find the key to
before they can cross over.

I am a guardian at the gate
holder of secrets, reminder of history
keeper of words:

one must remember silence
and learn when not to speak.

Musician

It began with five strings
on the back of my neck.

He was not from the sea,
nor stars of sky:
a master of wood
from an unlined note book,
he knew how to
use his hands to speak.

He knew by looking through a glass of vodka
a minor distance to be played
by pure instinct
he knew
listening to Latin songs,
laments from Cuba.

His body fluid from dancing
with you and you and you….

In the silver lights of rain
and constellation flute,
he knew I was made in haste,
made of the temporal,
made to always wait, out of tune,
without a band, without a pick.

He held me at the base line.
He held me alone after everyone
else had gone to the shelf,
case by case put away.

He played me.

Eros in Waiting

kiss shaped tiny as a flower
arrived in the mail

I dreamt it was from you
a cool thousand miles away

to cover my lips a bright yellow
full of hopeful bee pollen

tender as silk against my eyes
until I am certain I've fallen

as the last drop of dew
with the rising warmth of afternoon

whispering your name
small, round, and maroon

Epitaph

at the speed
of light

they loved hard
and fast

when beloved
to beloved

was not so far
as the moon

under the stone
of an angel face

painted in blue
shades

of their past
      here lies

Jupiter
and his mistress

in a woven
cocoon

Changing Positions of Light

Your last words plunge to their knees
and I remember the importance of small things.

I find a pack of matches you left behind.
I light one after the other and let them burn
until each flame goes out.

Not one is the same…
they each have their own style of smoke
and last just long enough
to share the light.

Clay Twist of Face

I am not the shape of a circle,
a square or anything wholesome.

I have always been as I am: anonymous
and perhaps drunk on the sound of a mantra;

on the song your name creates spilling
in a splash of light on your face.

I am not noble, tiered or grand.
Between my heart and head are devas,

demons that cry for want in the night:
hidden rivers, water wheels and rapids rushing.

Here beside me in my imagination
your eyes are closed in the jewels of sea.

I do not ask you to awaken or speak.
I do not ask you to teach me.

I would rather drop, plunge,
sink to the depths where you sleep.

Fragrance

You sway through the world
of handshakes and mochas
smelling of sugar cane
like sweetness
to anyone.

I wish to capture
the neo scent of your pure body
chiseled ochre of jukebox
sports car and anxious zest
that mingles with spiced rose
of jasmine in musk

left open like moody novels
on a bed of vodka and tiny deaths
as the only remains of our seduction
coloring the linen sheets
we shared.

Twilight

My lover has a passion
for hybrid orchids.

My house he fills
with blossoms stained magenta.

Bittersweet

everything curves in our dreams
   without straight lines

our slender waists and thighs
   curl in the blue sheets

already the lantern of desire
   is extinguished in sleep

lifeless without motion as if
   the breath between us has died

and only the absent moon knows
   the secrets she has stolen

tonight buried in the center
   of a passing cloud

in the heart we move
   undiluted, uninhibited, unedited

abandoned again in this moment
   where even in death

our bodies braided in linen
   belongs to me

flowers plucked from the road

*Come! Let's go see
the real flowers...
of this painful world.
Basho*

From the Center

a path opens to me
and unfolds the same as birth
only this time I hope
to emerge painted in the colors
of wisdom
before I am recycled again
into the earth

Sudden

without an end
    I am tore open again

as clouds separate
    to release rain

we rise and fall
  defy death

walk on tightropes
    aware of the nets

we shift our bodies
    as contours
      as particles

move in high velocity
    from dark to light
      from unreal to real

as lips on lips
    before speech
after the silence

    evaporates
      into
    your kiss

Supple as the Wind

It is written in the sutras that love
is of immeasurable equanimity
rather than darkness.

So, when the gossips come again
to share their empty words

I will tell them
talking is not communication
and from the hollow of their mouths
words do not heal -

except for example:

> *I love you.*

Wishing Tree in Delhi

I tie my handkerchief
and chunnis to this holy tree
just outside the temple
where it is okay to cry
for a secret thing
rather than let it burn inside
a lamp of desire.

Here

Your father's hand covers my navel
as I curl into the muscle of thigh.

We go on then…
kissing you into living,
into dying.

No Pity in This Poem

I know how I was created
and it is the same as you
with hands that fumbled in the dark
searching for music
and the comfort of belonging.

I don't mind the obvious:
that exposed marrow of a rejected
moment blown across the sand
and used like an excuse to get drunk
mean and full of sorrow.

We are only as cracked or as whole
as anybody we know -
full of clichés and panting
all in the same time zone.

It just depends on far one will go
to drop their face,
take off those silly pretensions
and dance holy naked
above the mundane
of anything too important…

*and become one with the madness
of being absolutely nothing.*

Panoramic

After the survival
of target practice, fire, floods
and some cruel words -
the silence of a prism
passes through flesh and decay
in the throat of a black hole
spits in spirals
for an early sun
peels back the edge
of a new landscape
where we find ourselves
naked as sound.

Courage

The still point that carries water
like a prayer

regardless of how many hearts
it borrows
or how often it travels
through the bodies of others
its presence rises
from the same vertigo
that creates both your heaven
and your sorrow

then settles in the memory
of small things
until the feeling of being
is stronger the need to control.

Damaged Poetry

The trouble with damaged poetry
is it is persistent, irresistible
and without resolution.

It is the prayer, perfume
and hang over. It is a feather
that slips through my mind
and floats away.

It is a black candle
and the red flames of goddesses
I have never met.

It is a crucifix
nailed on every page with new intentions
and mantras that heal with sound
but I cannot manage to write it
much less recite it.

A damaged poem is a late train
the confused marriage and
a horrible dinner with too much spice.
It is peanuts crushed on the floor
and zodiacs that fall from the sky.

Addicted I continue on
for the next feeling of belonging
for the next fix of awareness

in the moment when my eyes water
and I am lost again

inside the perfect damage
of someone else…

where I find myself
on the cusp of light
perched on the edge of insight
where your voice
drops between the lines
of intimate gravity
like Galileo's orange.

Impressionism

Whistler, Sargent, Cassatt
and Madame X
had something in common
besides paint,
pastels, powered flesh
free time and wandering
in the City of Light.

They had the desire
to capture rare beauty
in all of its insolent persistence
and transform the offensive
detestable, swarthy and rebellious
into translucent strokes
of those who dared
to transcend.

Still Life: Oil on Linen

Left open on a table are cracked oysters
and dark shells of indigo in suggestion.

From this distance they look like butterflies
on a fence in hushed expectancy
without the sentient need for evanescence –

they fly in the sepia tone field of bones
exploring the unknown.

Autumn

last in the kitchen
after a tropical night of storms and fireflies
with a ribbon loose
on her small freckled shoulder
she yawns and pours a cup of juice

beside a sexy girl
blushing over the attention
her accent gives her
when someone breaks the bread:

So, who was moaning last night?
God, that was a good one, eh?

we all thought it was Summer
until Autumn spilt her juice

Island Goddess

vines were tangled in your hair when you arrived
naked in leaves of tea with bare feet and toe rings:
a fresh fruit fallen from your mother's garden
with lips drawn on in mischief, circles of *Oh*
tongues tasted for innocent color, for the pallet
of mirth knowing now as you do of escape,
misbehaving and moon light serenading

Following the Stars Home

Nomads walk in seamless deserts
by touch of sand
in the smoke of pale cigarettes.

The trail of their journey
is on the brittle wind
and cracked salt of the lips.

A horizon blurs and sways
in stale coffee -
bodies are wrapped for a pyre
to journey with the stars home.

For the living:

sand washed prayers
to hang
on the vines of dreams
and air dry
under a mala of stars
between who we used to be
and who we are.

Let clouds disappear
into the sea -

and the moon drink
dark words from our lips
while we sleep.

Soft Cusp

My hands hold nothing in particular
except random scars that point to road signs
often too hard to find in the dark.

Now my hands only wish to touch
the soft cusp and rim of your changing eyes
across the meridians of the world
you have held in behind the cry.

Overture

Let prayer walk like a pilgrim
    with torn shoes and holy crumbs.

May the effigy of mute sparrows
    remain in our hearts...

        beautiful in love as I celebrate
the way we wore stars.

Pilgrim Hitchhiking on the Road of Life

I prefer your song to fill
the space between us.

I want every reason
you have for the spread of light
in humanity...
to share
what I hear in your plea
for love.

I desire your kind of magic
as you dance or stumble
through transformation.

Your supplication
of wisdom, freedom and
transcendence always just
out of reach.

Your fragile voices of
unmitigated sorrow
and small wonders
discovered in the blue darkness
that holds the stars
in a great expanse of mystery
     an uncanny faith.

In your face I see myself
full of love's attachments.

Now here is my gratitude
for sharing this road
of phenomena,
where I too am lost sometimes
in the unknown

in hands of prophecy
wild fools, tarot and the Tao.

Let's remember to be gentle...

for I am abandoned to your song
as a first and last kiss
of immense awareness
while our lives
circle around each other
to meet again at the crossroads.

When I Die

when I disappear completely
and I can no longer call out your name

when I cannot kiss you
or run my moist tongue along the sweetness
of you and my lips are blue from the cold

when my fingers cannot touch you
and our shadows no longer compete for space
and my voice does not reach you

perhaps it is then we will know
each other for the first time

A Blind Path

By morning it will be too late
so we walk together
in darkness
not depending on mystics
planets or holy texts.

In a final hour
our only dream
is the hand of synchronicity
that keeps us warm
in love for each other.

At Ugly's Saloon

Drunk and demanding
he pulled the plug on the jukebox
since he had just met a Shaman
on blue mountain summoning
the medicine of whatever it takes
to create balance.

He said, "It is time our bodies become
containers of Spirit
to carry dreaming hearts back
to their owners,
otherwise we will not live long enough
to drink in the Rain Dance."

Healing Hands

Javier used to play poker
and drink his dice
like worms
under the canopy of a Mexican sun
until his hands caught on fire
and started to burn.

Now he cools them
by touching the pain
of others -
an ace of light
healing the loss
and hurt.

Ban-cha (toasted green tea)

In fields of bamboo
the legend is this:

out of the sea rose Nuika
a queen with a dragon tail
to cure the world by fire
but she forgot an important detail
so the sky has cracks
and is wide open in duality.

Now we have only this cup
in the evanescence of dreams
…it is up to us to heal.

We close our eyes and sip
slowly from a broken heaven.

Situational Perspective

Chisel the light off my skin
and bottle it

because I have eight truths
for love and beauty;
for loyalty and eternity.

And, I wonder why
the mind writes the world
in complete Requiem
huddled in browns, colored in shadows
mostly windblown -
war torn and confused
in the hues of a bruise?

Speed of Love

I am inside
your solitary world
where you are a pure number
without records

or memories
to acknowledge gravity.

I transform
and push time back
into a corner

so there is no death
at this velocity

as fast as you can push it…

I go straight to your head
yielding to curves
of Divinity

…transverse destiny

to cross over
the black and white
finish line of your heart.

The Great Wall of China

It comes as a surprise to find that
the Great Wall of China divides
you and I.

Forgive me as I wander into the blue houses
of our past, remembering the places we loved to go.

You tell me not to take it so seriously
but I will not forget the harmony
or the pilgrimage of our hearts.

There is no simple solution to deliver us from the ruins.
Yet, classic beauty will remain.

And I know what we have done
while mastering the difficulty of traveling
the Silk Road.

Gambling odds dictate a winner's or loser's fate
and probably they will say to me that a thousand miles of wall
cannot be removed…

but I will never give up in believing that it can.

Street Monk

on the streets
to leave behind what he knows
in scandal or just to be away

with a guitar and duffel bag
in dirty bus stops
he drinks to the void
and gives God a salute
without favors or free clothes

he tosses valuables
so no one will ask him
for answers to what he wants to forget

he prefers to die alone
in a strange city
rather than explain anything to this world
with her final demands
and bitter practice of stealing air
from death row

it is easier to let go
of iconoclasts and obscenities
to live off blasphemies
with a mouthful of smoke

he won't hold his breath
waiting for life to apologize
for the insane, mad and cruel

his advice: neither should you

Just This, Only This

Follow the blue smoke
that rolls off a beat poet's tongue
to the road along a heliotrope sentence
slower than worn skin
where the sagebrush burns
on the edge of another ellipse.

Imagine the promise
of boundaries devoured by evening

to erase details hidden dreams
that swell above dark waters
and lift a soul away from chaos
from the rim of madness.

No one can give you the truth
but you will go on to seek it.

Who or what was caught
in the bright colors of dawn?
Or was it just a state of mind
to anchor a body in bardo?

It could have been eight temptations
before sunrise...

No one is certain:

except we know it is almost winter
as our shadows fill in the space of zero
and everyone goes home in a setting sun.

Dissolving

Loose as crystals
tiny refractions
of light

    I fall

into a slow spiral
as my impurities slip
into fusion.

I escape
through pure coalescence

make an exodus
stripped without color
of the pensive and oppressed.

I spill into a swirl
of expansion -
a rush of split molecules.

    I melt

as a milky way
of matter liquefied
into a sweet viscous union.

God takes all of me
right here
in the middle of the afternoon.

Translucent

   After the exile of hope

       I rise

   spilling light from a body
   dressed without the years.

Pinholes

Right, like you believe me anyway
but I could see the light
on the other side of heaven
through those pinholes
in the sky.

You might argue
that heaven is a myth
but I saw the curve of darkness
wrap its long legs
around the length of light.

They were kissing each other
right in the center
of existence.

It really doesn't matter
that God owns the copyright
to the most popular book on Earth
or that the Devil wears designer clothes

or that I cannot describe
the map of my soul
and its perimeters of love.

What matters is we sleep in
this world of dreams
and gather the strength we need
to dive into what is real.

The Heart Moves into the Body

This time you cannot have it all your way.

If you want to hang your heart
somewhere that really cares
then you need to listen when it speaks
and give up the idea that you are separate
just because the body might complain
or carry pain longer than you think it should.

It is true that you have to come clean
about those affairs
of being not what you are meant to be.

Just think of all the places
you and your heart have yet to go;
all of the uncharted love
just waiting to be discovered.

Journey of the Magi

My face is unfinished
and shoulders bent
as an old tree in winter.

In the hanging gardens
behind the broken
locks of temple gates

I searched for miracles
with the dryness of incense
and purple ash.

I watched the bodies burn bodies
turn graves and give birth again.

Nomads, thieves and merchants
held out their hands
waiting for the light to rise;
waiting for the humility
that comes after everything
has been taken away.

I found myself
in the beggar woman
and in the rose
only to fold like paper in the wind.

I saw actions turn back to their source
curl in the corners as reminders
between who I am, have been
and might not be.

Now I arrive home
to offer an embrace

knowing that the world
will go on spinning
without even remembering
our names.

And, it was going to rain…

in the early hours
when some bury their dead

on this branch
in the shades of gray

teach me how to love you
how to not die in slow installments
of eternity that inch closer

silence the sound of swords
give me the soft fabrics
of beauty in paintings

I will settle for dandelions
dogwood and rosemary on the winds
it doesn't matter if the sun has no news
or if an eclipse steals the moon

just let me cultivate the light
        (the sweet songs from your voice)
and bloom in the night like magnolia

Village Stories

Children's voices are heard in the roads
long after the lights go out
and mango leaves bend in the wind.

Their mothers call each one by name
in a language that sings of home
and speaks without violence.

After Midnight

Leaning over you body
I see the door of your heart is slightly open
left unattended by the guard
who went off with the maid to dance
in his dreams.

Someone should teach us
how to turn the beauty of our nights
into art that flirts in daylight
then we will not be surprised
by the sideways smiles or pink faces
left bare with shaky knees.

Sanctuary

You arrived in a dream
       and left the same way.

Part of me thought it was overblown
how you might just touch me
in one minute to change life as I knew it
and walk like a flower
among the thorns of my discolored heart.

The other part of me knew
it was you
      would always be you
to rise like a sweet fragrance
in the strangely lonesome field
I call "myself"
to populate it with love.

So, when I start to think it is dead
all dried up and gone
with the memories uprooted
and nothing to show for it
except a few seeds...

suddenly the selfless joy of our embrace
emerges like a rose in sunlight

…. and once again
    I am surrounded by our flowers
        in full bloom.

The Perfect Poem

In the cult of words
that curl around one another
like fetishes and pulp

between the last breath
of a metallic year
and the dream of blooming
in rebirth…

I did not find you
except in the calla lily
and the fire rose.

About the Author:

Zayra Yves is published in numerous print journals and on-line magazines: *The Zimbabwe Situation; The Panhandler Quarterly; Voices for Africa; Eyes of the Poet; Kreativ; Reflections IIT Madras (India); Edge Life Magazine; Poetry Life & Times*; *Astropoetica, 34th Parallel* and *Alehouse Press*. She has appeared as a featured guest on the West Marin Community Radio for "House of the Poet" and on SW Radio Africa's "Outside Looking In," as well as many other radio stations and on-line audio programs. Her audio poetry collections have appeared on *Integral Naked, TWiN, Perfectly Said, Mazungue Studio One, Zimvibes, Chicago's North Western University Radio, Woman's Radio, Radioindy and Coolfire*. Currently she lives in Northern California with her family.

Please visit Zayra's website for updates: www.zayrayves.com

www.ingramcontent.com/pod-product-compliance
Lightning Source LLC
Chambersburg PA
CBHW051804040426
42446CB00007B/503